Sportsmanship

by Michael Teitelbaum

Raintree

Chicago, Illinois

© 2004 Raintree

Published by Raintree, a division of Reed Elsevier, Inc.
Chicago, Illinois
Customer Service 888-363-4266
Visit our website at www.raintreelibrary.com

For information, address the publisher: Raintree, 100 N. LaSalle, Suite 1200, Chicago, IL 60602

Printed and bound in China.

08 07 06 05 04

10 9 8 7 6 5 4 3 2 1

Library of Congress Cataloging-in-Publication Data

Teitelbaum, Michael.
    Sportsmanship / Michael Teitelbaum.
        v. cm. — (Character education)
    Includes bibliographical references and index.
    Contents: What is sportsmanship? — Play fairly, play by the rules of the game — Avoid arguments — Be a team player — Everyone should get to play — Do your very best, always — Accept the judgment calls of game officials and show respect for those officials — Follow your coach's directions — Respect your opponent — Win without gloating — Lose without complaining — Remember, it's just a game.
        ISBN 0-7398-7008-4 (lib. bdg.-hardcover) — ISBN 1-4109-0327-3 (pbk.)
    1. Sportsmanship — Juvenile literature. [1. Sportsmanship.] I. Title. II. Character education (Raintree (Firm))
    GV706.3.T45 2004
    175 — dc21

                                                                            2003005855

A Creative Media Applications, Inc. Production
WRITER: Michael Teitelbaum
DESIGN AND PRODUCTION: Alan Barnett, Inc.
EDITOR: Susan Madoff
COPYEDITOR: Laurie Lieb

PHOTO CREDITS:
Cover: ©Bob Daemmrich / The Image Works
National Baseball Hall of Fame Library, Cooperstown, NY *page:* 5, 10
AP/Wide World Photographs *pages:* 6, 7, 9, 12, 13, 15, 17, 18, 19, 24, 25, 26, 27, 28, 29
2002 ARTTODAY.COM, INC., and its licensors. All rights reserved. *pages:* 8, 14
© Bettmann/CORBIS *page:* 11
© Reuters NewMedia Inc./CORBIS *page:* 16, 22
© Paul A. Souders/CORBIS *page:* 20
© Pete Saloutos/CORBIS *page:* 21
© Bill Greenblatt/Getty Images *page:* 23

Some words are shown in bold, **like this.** You can find what they mean by looking in the glossary.

Contents

What Is Sportsmanship?

"Sportsmanship for me is when a guy walks off the court and you really can't tell whether he won or lost, when he carries himself with pride either way."
—Professional tennis player Jim Courier

The dictionary defines sportsmanship as "the ability to take loss or defeat without complaint, and the ability to accept victory without **gloating.**" People who exhibit sportsmanship treat their opponents with fairness, **generosity, respect,** and courtesy.

People who exhibit sportsmanship believe that playing fairly, sticking to the rules, and doing their very best are more important than the final score. Nobody likes to lose, but learning how to lose **graciously,** whether in sports or in life, is a sign of strong character.

Winning graciously is equally important. When you shake hands with a losing player, or with members of the losing team, and congratulate them for their hard work and fair play, you're being a good winner.

A great sportsman

In 1900 a pitcher named Christy Mathewson helped bring sportsmanship to the rough world of baseball. Baseball players in the early part of the century were rowdy and impolite. They shouted at fans and at each other throughout the games. Polite, well-read, and a strong believer in fair play, Mathewson encouraged his teammates to play with the same values.

Pitcher Christy Mathewson helped bring sportsmanship to the game of baseball.

As other players followed Mathewson's example, baseball became a spectator sport enjoyed by the whole family. Mathewson was so respected for his sportsmanship that on October 5, 1901, he was asked to umpire a game he played in!

Sportsmanship, Not Gamesmanship

There are two different attitudes an athlete can bring to playing a sport or game. One is called sportsmanship— the other is called gamesmanship.

Players who believe that winning is all that matters show gamesmanship, not sportsmanship. They may find a way to bend or break the rules in order to gain an edge in competition.

Displaying good sportsmanship while visiting another school is one way to show pride in your own school.

Players who believe that *how* you play the game is more important than winning show sportsmanship, not gamesmanship. They believe that the real victory comes with competing fairly and **respecting** opponents and teammates. They are willing to lose rather than play unfairly.

On the road

It is important to display sportsmanship, not gamesmanship, when your team travels to another school to play a game. Whether you are an athlete playing in the game or a fan in the bleachers rooting for your school, you should have respect for your school and be proud of it. The best way to really display that pride is to show respect for the players and fans of the other school's team. By acting with sportsmanship, you reflect well on your own school.

"Sportsmanship is a way of life that every athlete and person in society should uphold. Sportsmanship is the ability to understand and respect one another's ability no matter what the situation is."

—Marion Jones, Olympic track-and-field gold medalist

Play Fairly, Play by the Rules of the Game

A player competing in a sporting event has to understand the rules to know how to play the game. But it takes sportsmanship to always play by those rules.

Playing fairly and following the rules are more important than winning. Honesty and **integrity** are important parts of sports and sportsmanship. Players who bring those values to the field are always winners.

Playing fairly and by the rules is more important than the final score.

Rather than accept a victory that he felt was earned unfairly, the coach of the Arsenal soccer team of London called for a rematch.

Winning by cheating is not winning at all. If your team ends the game with a winning score but failed to follow the rules then the score is meaningless. A true winner always exhibits sportsmanship.

"Thanks, but no thanks"

In a 1999 British soccer game between Arsenal of London and Sheffield United, the coach and members of the Arsenal team refused to accept a 2–1 victory because they felt that their own winning goal was scored unfairly. Even though game officials would have allowed the goal to count, and even though taking the win would have improved the team's record for the season, they did not want to win by unfair means. It was decided that the two teams would play a rematch.

The sportsmanship displayed by the Arsenal team showed that playing fairly and by the rules was more important than just winning.

Arguing with officials, coaches, or opponents accomplishes nothing. It gets in the way of doing your best. It also prevents you from staying focused on the game.

During the course of a game, things might not go your way. Sometimes an official may make a call that you disagree with. Sometimes your coach might make a decision that you think is wrong. Sometimes your opponent does something that you think is unfair.

Arguing in any of these situations will not change the previous play. It will only disrupt the game. Stay committed to doing your best, and get ready for the next play.

Jackie Robinson broke baseball's color barrier by having the courage and sportsmanship not to fight when opposing players mistreated him.

The courage not to fight

In 1947 Jackie Robinson joined the Brooklyn Dodgers and broke baseball's color barrier to become the first African American to play major-league baseball in the 20th century. His sportsmanship in the face of **racism,** and threats from fans, managers, opposing players, and even his own teammates, allowed him to accomplish this difficult task.

Baseball executive Branch Rickey signs a major-league baseball contract with Jackie Robinson. Rickey knew that Robinson displayed the sportsmanship needed to avoid fighting and to successfully open the door for African-American players in the major leagues.

Despite the terrible things that were said to him, Robinson controlled his temper, avoided arguments and fights, and focused on playing the game. His sportsmanship and strength of character helped make certain that players of all races would play together in professional sports.

Be a Team Player

In any team sport each member of the team must work with the others for the team to be successful. If you **respect** your teammates, the entire team benefits. Your behavior reflects on the team, and your individual success is an important contribution to the team effort.

Praise your teammates when they do well, and comfort and encourage them when they make mistakes. Never **criticize** your teammates, even if their mistakes result in a loss. Unity, support, and teamwork are key parts of sportsmanship.

"I've worked too hard and too long to let anything stand in the way of my goals. I will not let my teammates down, and I will not let myself down."

—Mia Hamm, member of the U.S. Women's World Cup soccer team

Amir Hadad and Aisam Ul-Haq Qureshi played together as teammates despite their different backgrounds.

Working together

If you play on a team, you may have teammates from different backgrounds, places, races, or religions. Accepting and working with them all is part of teamwork and good sportsmanship.

At the Wimbledon tennis tournament in 2002, two players who could not have been more different teamed up to play together as doubles partners. Aisam Ul-Haq is from Pakistan and is a member of the Muslim faith. His partner, Amir Hadad, is from Israel and is a member of the Jewish faith. Although there have been conflicts between the countries and religions of these two men, they played together as teammates and set an example for the whole world.

The concept of being on a team means that everyone pitches in to help the team do its best. This means that everyone should get a chance to play. Each player, regardless of skill level, deserves to play because he or she is a member of the team. A player who shows good sportsmanship wants everyone to share in the victory or defeat and to do it as a team.

Everyone on the team should get a chance to play.

Do the right thing

Here is a story to think about. It is late in a youth league soccer game, and Jane, the last player on the bench, is the only one who has not played. The score is tied, and the team would like to have its best players on the field to try to win the game. This means that Jane would not get to play in this game. What is the right thing for the coach to do? Should Jane be put in the game?

"Do you know what my favorite part of the game is? The opportunity to play."

—Mike Singletary, Hall of Fame professional football player

In this story the teammates agreed that Jane should be allowed to play. They decided that allowing everyone to **participate** is much more important than the final score. Perhaps Jane might assist in scoring a goal or score one herself. It is important to remember that you win or lose as a team.

Whether you are at practice or playing a championship game, you can display sportsmanship by giving your very best effort at all times. That way you'll always feel good about yourself regardless of the game's outcome. Whether you're the star of the team or a supporting player, you'll know that you were fully prepared for the game and that you contributed to the best of your

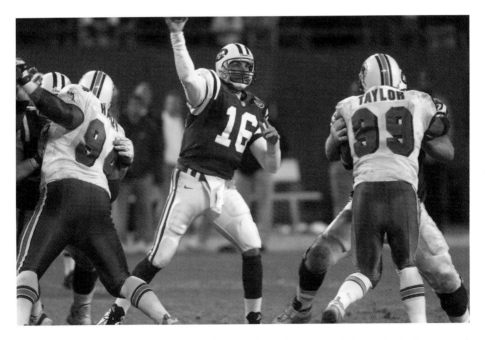

Even though they trailed by 23 points, the New York Jets did their very best and came back to win the game.

abilities. Whether you are playing to get some exercise or joining a pickup game with friends or competing in an organized youth sports league, doing your best is another way to show your sportsmanship.

"It ain't over..."

Hall of Fame catcher Yogi Berra once said about a baseball game, "It ain't over till it's over." Berra meant that players should never give up. They should always continue to do their very best, even if there is a big difference in the score.

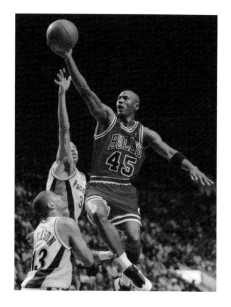

"I can accept failure. Everyone fails at something. But I can't accept not trying."

—Professional basketball player Michael Jordan

In October 2000 the New York Jets trailed the Miami Dolphins by a score of 30–7 in the fourth quarter of a football game. The Jets did not give up. They knew that to make a comeback they had to continue to do their best on every single play. The Jets rallied to tie the game and send it into overtime. In the early hours of the next morning, the Jets finally won by a score of 40–37.

Respecting game officials is an important part of exhibiting sportsmanship.

The people who work as officials at games are human, too. Even though they sometimes make mistakes, you must **respect** their judgments and follow their rulings. Officials try hard to be fair, but sometimes they see a play from a different angle than the players or coaches. It is important to accept their calls and move on to the next play.

Officials have been trained to do their jobs, and they understand the rules. As part of a team, you must always accept the fact that the officials have the final say. Arguing with officials wastes time and effort and displays poor sportsmanship. Officials are there for the good of the game. Show them respect and accept their calls.

Take a bow

Baseball has been played in Japan since 1873. There, players follow a tradition that shows great sportsmanship. Before coming up to the plate to bat, Japanese baseball players bow to their opponents. Then they bow to the umpires. Bowing is a traditional sign of respect in East Asia. The players bow to show respect for the officials, for the other team, and for the history of baseball.

Japanese baseball players bow out of respect for the game, their opponents, and the officials.

Your job as a member of a team is to be committed to doing your best. Your coach's job is to help the team display its best effort. A player who shows good sportsmanship trusts the coach's advice, directions, and experience.

Sometimes giving up individual glory helps your team win the game.

You may not always agree with what the coach says or does. A decision the coach makes may not be as good for you as for another player. But the coach has to think about the best interests of every player on the team. Coaches are always thinking about the big picture—the entire team.

Sacrifice

Think about this situation. You are a power hitter on your baseball team. In one particular game, your team has a runner on first base

*Teamwork includes following the coach's directions
even if you disagree with his or her plans.*

with no outs. Your team trails by one run. Your coach calls
on you to lay down a sacrifice bunt—a softly hit ball—to
advance the runner on first base into scoring position.
You would rather swing hard, hoping to smack a two-run
home run and be a hero. But your coach is thinking
about the overall good of the team. The coach is asking
you to give up your shot at individual glory to work as part
of a team and to help get a run.

Your team is counting on you to do what the coach asks
without question or complaint. Following your coach's
directions puts the team's best interests ahead of your own.

Whether the team or individual you are playing against wins or loses, all opponents deserve **respect** for their efforts. You exhibit sportsmanship when you show **appreciation** for your opponents.

Let's shake on it!

Little League baseball players learn to respect their opponents. When the game is over, players from both teams line up and walk past each other to shake hands.

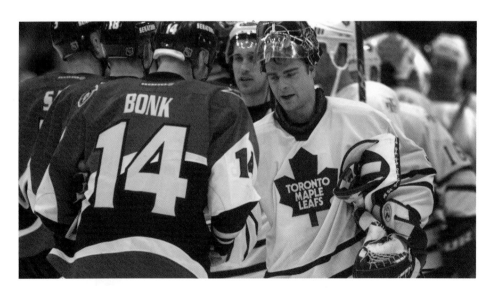

NHL players also shake hands after a playoff series game to say thanks for competing fairly and playing a good game.

This is a chance to say thank you for playing a good game.

After each National Hockey League (NHL) play-off series game, players from both teams line up on the ice and skate past each other. Again, each player has the chance to shake hands with everyone on the opposing team, offering thanks for a good game.

Throughout their friendly competition for the home run record, Sammy Sosa and Mark McGwire showed great respect for each other.

The chase

Chicago Cubs outfielder Sammy Sosa was especially **gracious** during his 1998 home-run chase with Mark McGwire. Both Sosa and McGwire were close to beating Roger Maris's record of 61 home runs, the most ever in one season. The friendly home-run battle went back and forth for the whole season.

When McGwire broke the record, his team was playing against the Cubs. Sammy Sosa leaped into McGwire's arms to congratulate him. Sosa was thrilled that his rival in the race had achieved his goal, even though he succeeded in breaking the record before Sosa did.

A true sportsman does not let competition come between friends.

Everyone has lost a game. It can be a disappointing and frustrating experience. When you are on the winning team, do not brag about it to the losing team. Shake hands and praise your opponents for a good effort. In many cases, your opponent may also be your friend. Do not let being a bad winner cause harm to your friendships.

It is fine to feel pride in your victory, but not at the expense of putting down someone else. You could just as easily be on the losing side tomorrow! Winning gracefully is one of the truest signs of sportsmanship.

Sweetness

Until recently, Hall of Fame National Football League running back Walter Payton was the league's all-time leading rusher. Payton, nicknamed "Sweetness," was one of the greatest football players to play the game.

Payton scored a total of 125 touchdowns and never once spiked the ball after a score (spiking the ball, or throwing it hard at the ground, is a traditional way to express happiness on the field). He did not want to show up his opponents or **gloat** about his **achievement.** He simply scored, flipped the ball to the official, and went back to playing the game. Payton was **respected** for his sportsmanship by his teammates, his opponents, and game officials.

All-time football great Walter Payton never gloated
or made his opponents feel bad about his success.

Lose Without Complaining

It is just as important to know how to be a good loser as it is to be a good winner. Do not make excuses, get angry, or sulk. Learn from your mistakes, practice, and get ready for the next game. True sportsmanship lies in your ability to accept the final score, whether the outcome is a winning or a losing one. Good sports take pride in doing their very best and do not grumble or whine when they lose a game.

Even though they lost, the Little League team from Harlem was proud to have reached the World Series and to have done its very best.

Moving past disappointment

In the 2002 Little League World Series, the team from Harlem in New York City played against the team from Worcester, Massachusetts, in the United States semifinal round. The Harlem team

"Winning is the easy part, losing is really tough. But you learn more from one loss than you do from a million wins."

—Olympic swimmer Amy Van Dyken

lost and was eliminated from the tournament even though the players gave it their best effort.

Despite their disappointment in not winning, the boys from Harlem showed great sportsmanship by waking up early the very next morning and taking part in a home-run hitting contest with players from all teams. The Harlem players did not complain about losing. They were proud to have **participated** in the World Series tournament and to have put forth their best effort.

You should always compete to the best of your ability. But win or lose, when the game is over the important thing is that you **participated** and had some fun with the other players—both teammates and opponents. **Gloating** about a win or sulking about a loss ruins the day for everyone. When the game is over, shake hands, smile, and move on.

Sportsmanship is about leaving the field with a sense of satisfaction and pride whether you have won or lost the game.

"For many of us who struggle with 'fitting in' or our identity, sports gives us our first face of confidence. That first bit of confidence can be a gateway to many other great things!"

—Olympic decathlete Dan O'Brien

Remember to also display good sportsmanship off the field. Do not let something that happened during a game harm friendships once the game is over. The elements needed for good sportsmanship in the game—fairness, **generosity, respect,** courtesy, and winning and losing **graciously**—are just as important off the field.

Glossary

achievement accomplishment or success

appreciation understanding the value of people or things

criticize to point out someone's faults

generosity willingness to share and give unselfishly

gloating bragging or teasing a losing player about the fact that you won

graciously with politeness and gentleness

integrity behaving with honesty and according to a code of ethics

participate to join or take part in a game or activity

racism prejudice against people based on the color of their skin

respect high regard for another person

Adler, C.S. *Winning.* New York: Clarion Books, 1999.

A thirteen-year-old girl who is trying to make her school's tennis team must deal with a teammate who wants her to cheat in order to succeed.

Bowen, Fred. *Winners Take All.* Atlanta, Ga.: Peachtree Publishers, 2000.

When a twelve-year-old baseball player lies about a catch he made, he is forced to decide which is more important—winning or sportsmanship.

Hallinan, P.K. *Let's Play As a Team.* Nashville, Tenn.: Ideals Children's Books, 2001.

When a group of children argue over which game to play at recess, they must all exhibit sportsmanship in order to come together and decide what to do as a team.

Index